Contents

Unit 1 Hide-and-Seek

■ **Listen to the story.**   ■ **Listen and circle.**

Cat and Dog are playing in a castle.
They are playing hide-and-seek.

1

Cat is it.
"I will count to ten. One, two, three, four..."

cat

2

Dog goes into a **gold** room.

3

gold

There is a **web** in the corner.

4

web

Dog goes into a big **bo**x.

5

box

The box is **under** the table.

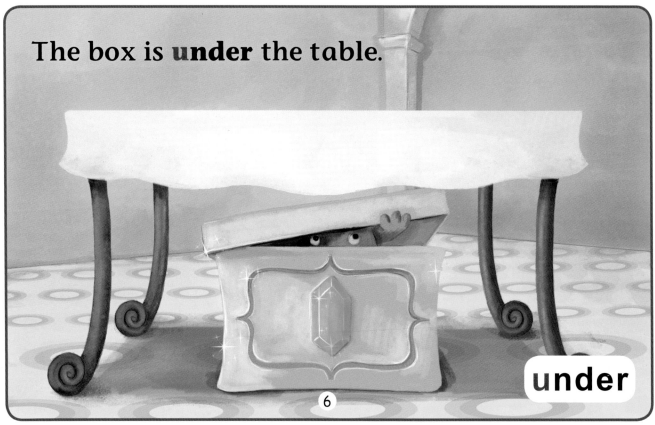

6

under

**Dog gets hungry.
His stomach makes a BIG sound.**

hungry

Cat finds Dog!

1 Consonants **c** & **g**

A Listen and repeat.

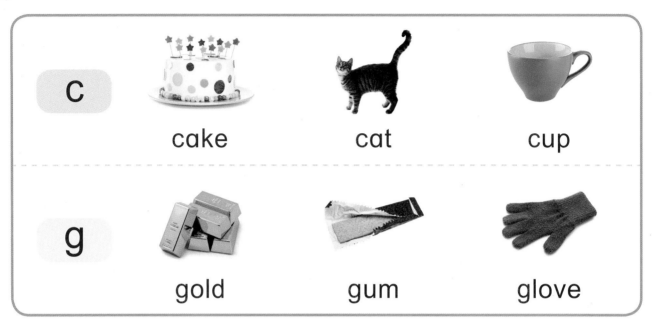

c

cake   cat   cup

g

gold   gum   glove

B Listen and circle the beginning letters.

1.

| c | g |

2.

| c | g |

3.

| c | g |

4.

| c | g |

5.

| c | g |

6.

| c | g |

C **Listen, write, and match.**

1.   cup

um

2.  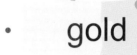 gold

up

3.  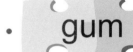 gum

old

4.  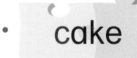 cake

ake

D **Listen and connect.**

1.

c um
g at

2.

c old
g ake

3.

c ake
g love

4.

c um
g an

5.

c love
g old

6.

c up
g et

E **Look, read, and circle.**

1.

cat

----

cup

2.

gold

----

gum

3.

glove

----

gum

4.

cake

----

cat

 F **Look and write.**

1.  ＿＿＿ + up → ＿＿＿＿＿

2.  ＿＿＿ + love → ＿＿＿＿＿

3.   ＿＿＿ + at → ＿＿＿＿＿

4.   ＿＿＿ + um → ＿＿＿＿＿

G Find and place the stickers.

c

g

H Look, circle, and write.

1.

cake   cat   cup

_C_____ is it. "I will count to ten."

2.

gum   gold   glove

_____

Dog goes into a _____ room.

A Listen and repeat.

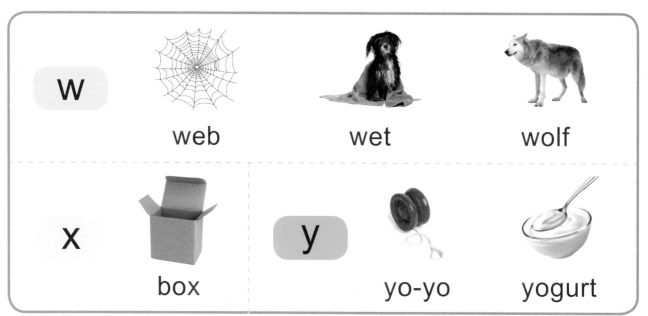

W

web　　　　wet　　　　wolf

X

box

y

yo-yo　　　yogurt

B Listen, number, and match.

◯ web　　◯ yogurt　　◯ box　　◯ wolf

·　　　　　·　　　　　·　　　　　·

·　　　　　·　　　　　·　　　　　·

C Listen, circle, and draw.

1. web wolf yo-yo box

2. wet box yogurt web

D Listen and solve the maze.

E Trace and write.

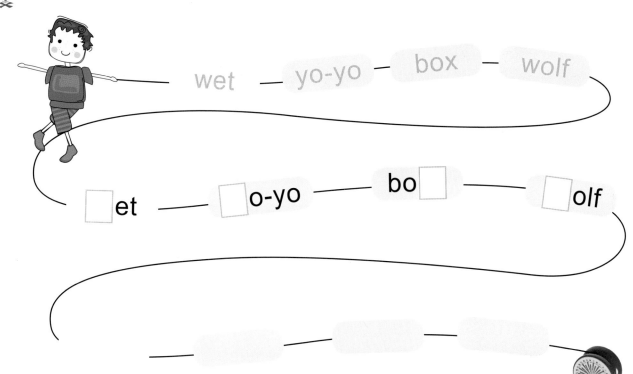

wet — yo-yo — box — wolf

☐et — ☐o-yo — bo☐ — ☐olf

F Look and trace.

1.

web   yo-yo

2.

wolf   box

3.

yogurt   wet

4.

yo-yo   web

G Find and place the stickers.

1.

2.

3.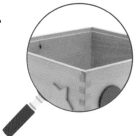

4.

H Look, circle, and write.

1.

wet   web   yogurt

There is a _____ in the corner.

2.

box   yo-yo   wolf

Dog goes into a big _____.

3 Short Vowel u

 A **Listen and repeat.**

u

umbrella   under   up

hungry   jump   run

B **Listen and number.**

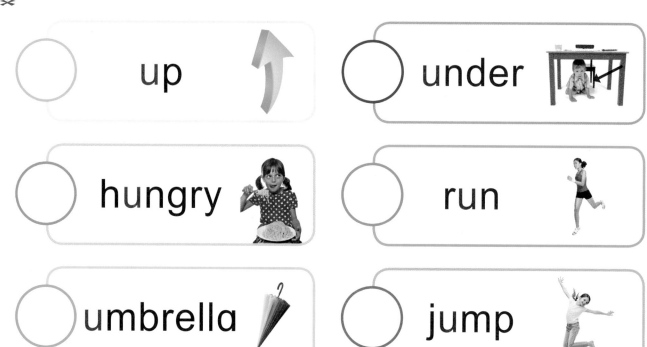

○ up

○ under

○ hungry

○ run

○ umbrella

○ jump

C **Listen and write.**

1.

_____ p

2.

h _ ngry

3.

_ mbrella

4.

j _ mp

5.

r _ n

6.

_ nder

D **Listen and circle.**

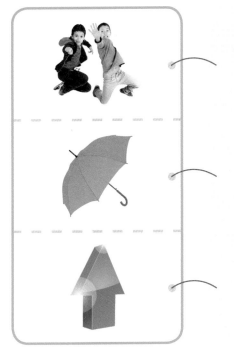

run   hungry   jump

jump   umbrella   up

up   under   hungry

E **Look, choose, and trace.**

1.    up   umbrella   under

2.    jump   hungry   run

3.    run   jump   under

 F **Look and write.**

1.

   u + ☐ → up

   + p →

2.

   + u + ☐ → run

   r + ☐ + n →

3.

   ☐ + u + ☐ + ☐ → jump

   j + ☐ + m + p →

up

under

u

jump

run

hungry

H **Look, circle, and write.**

1.

jump   under   run

The box is _____ the table.

2.

hungry   up   umbrella

Dog gets _____.

 **Unit 2** # A Day at the Beach

■ Listen to the story. ■ Listen and circle.

 T5

It's sunny and hot today.

1

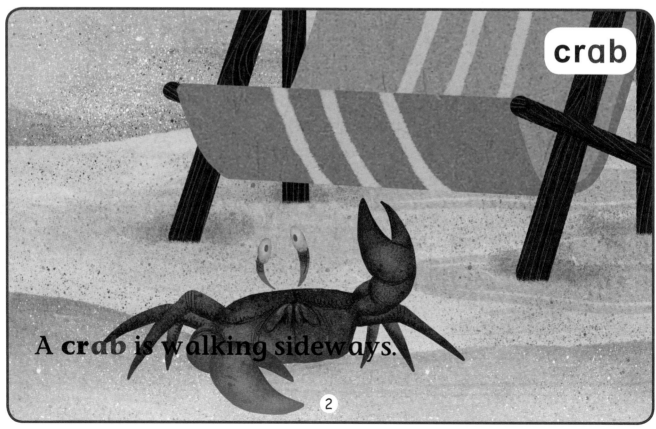

crab

A **crab** is walking sideways.

2

cap

A boy with **a** red **cap** is building a sandcastle.

3

man

A **man** is helping him build a big castle.

4

pants

A girl in blue **pants** is throwing a Frisbee.

5

wag

A dog is catching the Frisbee and **wag**ging his tail.

6

hat

A woman with a pink **hat** is picking up shells.

7

Everyone is enjoying the day at the beach.

8

1 Word Families -ab & -ap

A Listen and repeat.

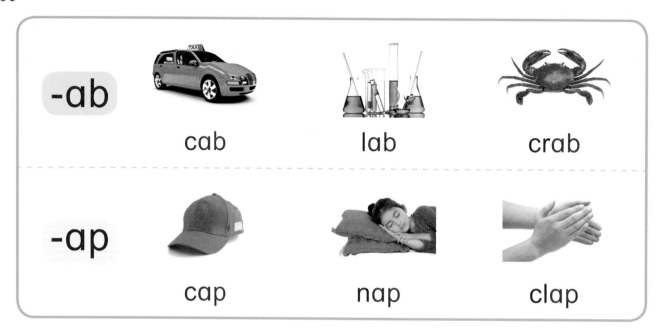

-ab

cab   lab   crab

-ap

cap   nap   clap

B Listen and circle.

1. crab

2. 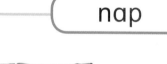 nap

3. lab

4. clap

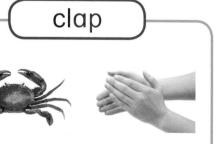

C Listen, find, and write.

1.

-ab

c _____

cr _____

| _____

2.

-ap

c _____

c| _____

n _____

cab   nap   lab   cap   crab   clap

D Listen, trace, and write.

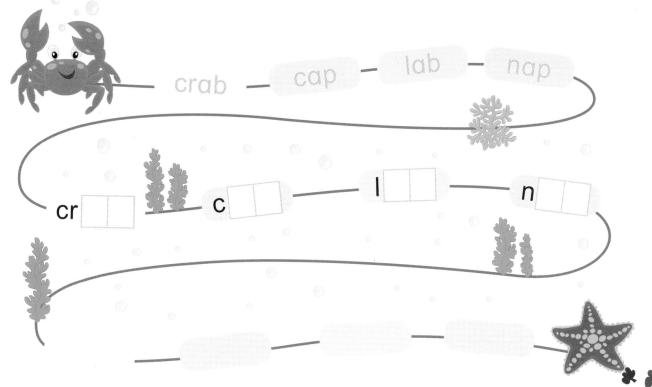

crab — cap — lab — nap

cr☐☐   c☐☐   l☐☐   n☐☐

E Look, choose, and trace.

1.  nap | cap

2. crab | cab

3. lab | cab

4. clap | nap

5. crab | lab

6. cap | clap

F Read and check.

1. It is a red crab.

☐ ☐

2. It is a red cap.

☐ ☐

3. He is in the lab.

☐ ☐

4. He is clapping.

☐ ☐

 G **Find and place the stickers.** stickers 1

1.

c

cr

2.

n

cl

H **Look, circle, and write.**

1.

cab   crab   lab

A _____ is walking sideways.

2.

cap   clap   nap

A boy with a red _____ is building a sandcastle.

2 Word Families -an & -ant

A Listen and repeat.

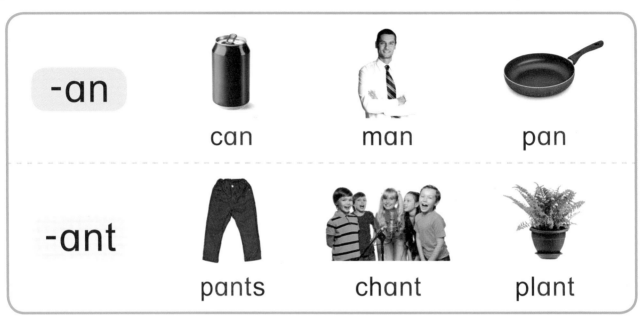

-an

can   man   pan

-ant

pants   chant   plant

B Listen, write, and match.

1. _____
   m _____ •

2. _____
   ch _____ •

3. _____
   p _____ •

4. _____
   pl _____ •

C Listen, find, and write.

1.

-an

_____

- - - - - - - - - - - - - - - -

_____

2.

-ant

_____

- - - - - - - - - - - - - - - -

_____

D Listen and solve the maze.

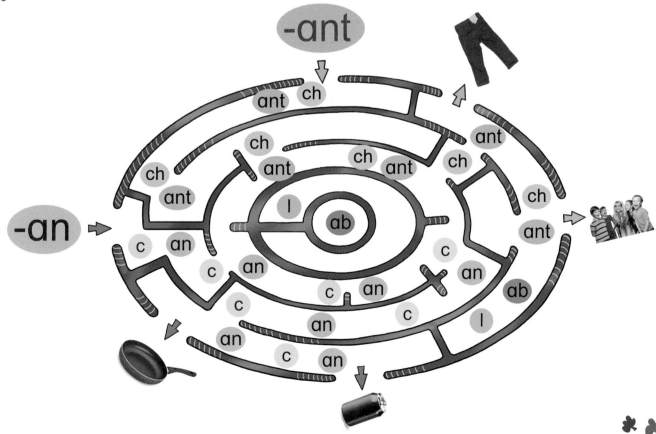

E Look and write.

1.

c + [ ] → can
[ ] + an → [ ]

2.

[ ] + ant → [ ]
pl + [ ] → plant

3.

[ ] + ant → [ ]
ch + [ ] → chant

4.

p + [ ] → [ ]
[ ] + an → pan

F Read and circle.

1. **-an** A (man) has a can and a pan.

2. **-ant** A man chants about pants and plants.

 G **Color the -an words in pink and the -ant words in blue.**

can	pants	
man		pan
	plant	chant

 H **Look, circle, and write.**

1.

   can   man   pan

   A _____ is helping him build a big castle.

2.

   pant   chant   plant

   A girl in blue _____s is throwing a Frisbee.

3 Word Families -ag & -at

A Listen and repeat.

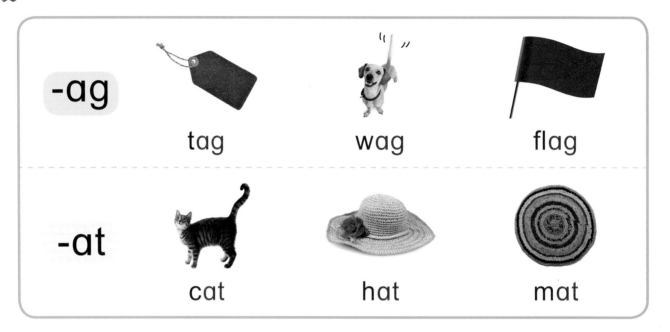

-ag

tag   wag   flag

-at

cat   hat   mat

B Listen and circle the same ending sounds.

1.

-ag

tag

cat

flag

2.

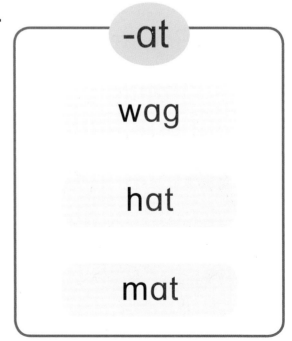

-at

wag

hat

mat

C Listen, find, and write.

1.

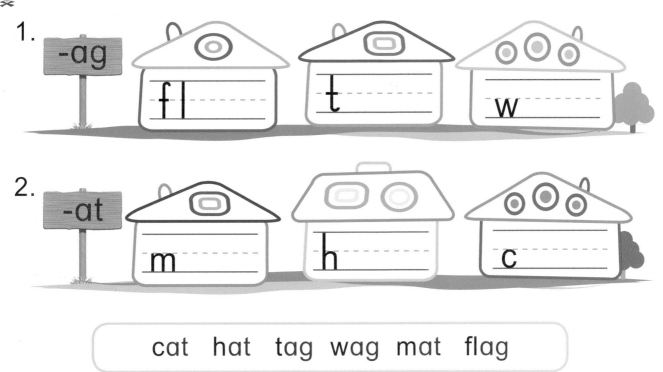

-ag

fl___   t___   w___

2.

-at

m___   h___   c___

cat   hat   tag   wag   mat   flag

D Listen, trace, and write.

tag   flag   hat   cat   t___   fl___

h___   c___

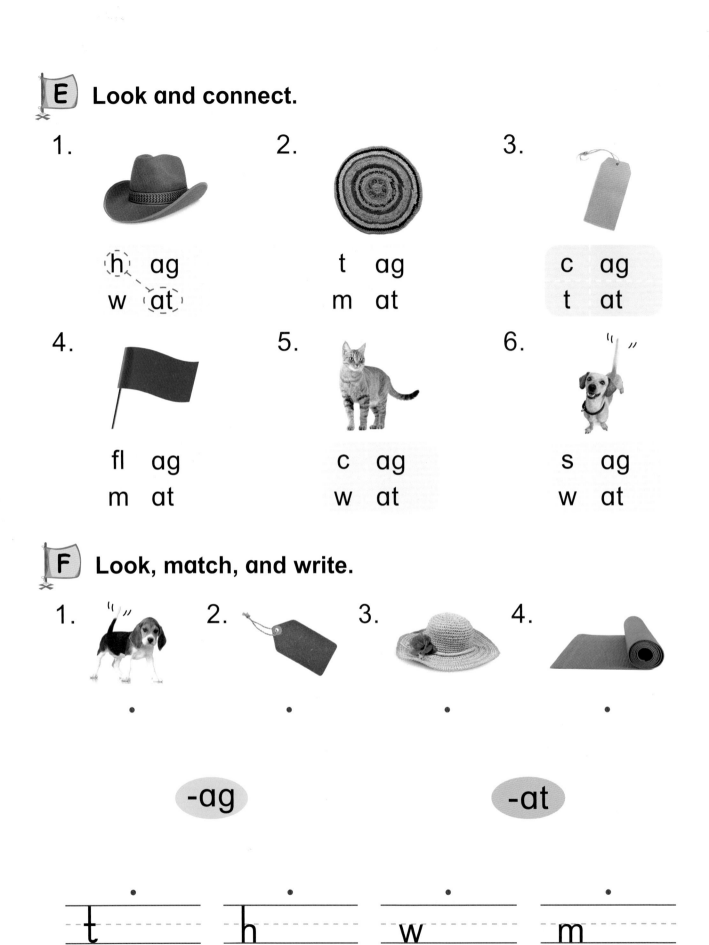

E **Look and connect.**

1.

h　ag
w　at

2.

t　ag
m　at

3.

c　ag
t　at

4.

fl　ag
m　at

5.

c　ag
w　at

6.

s　ag
w　at

F **Look, match, and write.**

1.　　2.　　3.　　4.

-ag　　　　　-at

t＿＿＿　　h＿＿＿　　w＿＿＿　　m＿＿＿

G **Find and place the stickers.** stickers 2

1.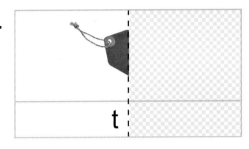
t

2.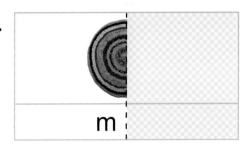
m

3.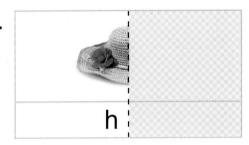
h

4.
fl

H **Look, circle, and write.**

1.

flag   tag   wag

_____

A dog is catching the Frisbee and _____ging his tail.

2.

hat   mat   cat

_____

A woman with a pink _____ is picking up shells.

 # It's the Holiday Season!

■ **Listen to the story.**　　■ **Listen and circle.** T9

Holiday music is everywhere in town.

1

You can see my **pet**, Happy, dancing to the music.

2

pet

You can see **ten** candy canes hanging on the tree.

ten

You can hear **bell**s ringing in the street.

bell

You can hear a bird singing in a **n**est.

⑤

nest

You can see Santa Claus flying in a **sl**ed.

⑥

sled

You can see white snow resting on the **twigs**.

7

twig

Everyone is happy!
The holiday spirit is everywhere!

8

1 Word Families -et & -en

A Listen and repeat.

-et

pet   net   wet

-en

ten   hen   den

B Listen and circle the ending sounds.

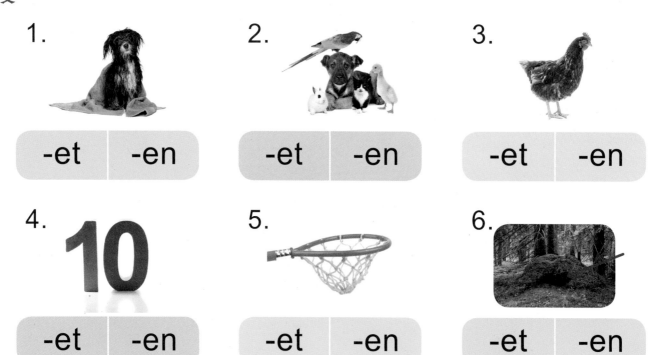

1.

-et   -en

2.

-et   -en

3.

-et   -en

4.

-et   -en

5.

-et   -en

6.

-et   -en

C **Listen, find, and write.**

1.

-et

n _____

p _____

w _____

2.

-en

t _____

d _____

h _____

net   den   pet   ten   wet   hen

D **Listen and circle.**

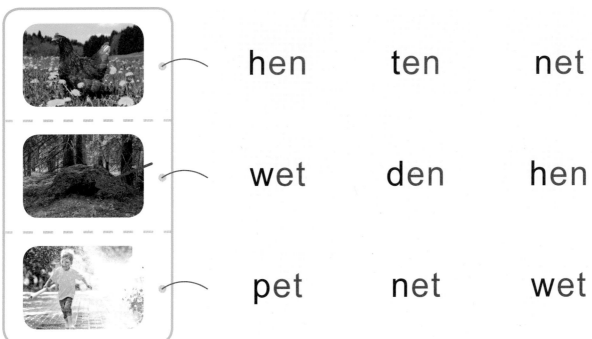

hen   ten   net

wet   den   hen

pet   net   wet

Look, read, and circle.

1.

net
pet

2.

hen
ten

3.

hen
den

4.

net
wet

 **Look, circle, and write.**

1.  d + en / et → _____

2.  n + en / et → _____

3.   t + en / et → _____

4.  p + en / et → _____

G **Find and place the stickers.**

-et

-en

H **Look, circle, and write.**

1.

pet   net   wet

You can see my _____, Happy, dancing to the music.

2.

den   hen   ten

You can see _____ candy canes hanging on the tree.

2 Word Families -ell & -est

T11

A Listen and repeat.

-ell

bell   well   shell

-est

nest   test   chest

B Listen, number, and match.

◯ bell   ◯ shell   ◯ chest   ◯ nest

C Listen, find, and write.

1.

-ell

_____

- - - - - - - - - - - -

_____

2.

-est

_____

- - - - - - - - - - - -

_____

D Listen and solve the maze.

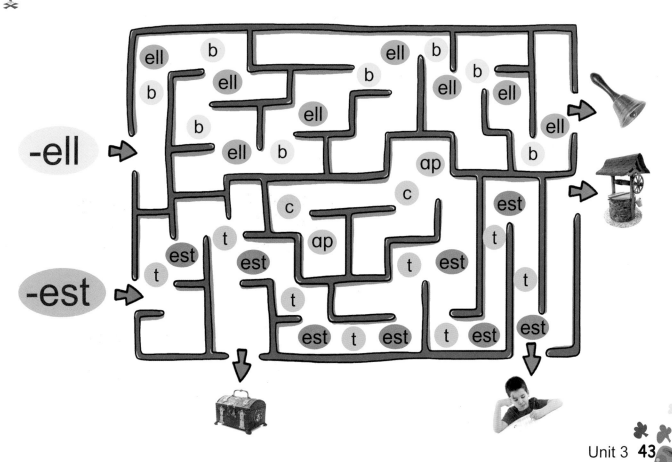

E Look, choose, and trace.

1.

   bell   shell   well

2.

   test   nest   chest

3.

   well   bell   shell

F Read and check.

1. It is a pink shell.

2. The gold is in the chest.

3. He has a test.

 G **Color the -ell words in pink and the -est words in blue.**

bell	shell	
test		nest
	well	chest

 H **Look, circle, and write.**

1.

   well   bell   shell

   You can hear _____s ringing in the street.

2.

   chest   nest   test

   You can hear a bird singing in a _____.

3 Word Families -ed & -ig

A Listen and repeat.

-ed

bed red sled

-ig

big pig twig

B Listen and match.

1. -ed • • big •

2. -ig • • red •

3. -ed • • pig •

4. -ig • • bed •

C Listen, find, and write.

1.

-ed

b

s|

r

2.

-ig

t w

p

b

| red | big | bed | pig | twig | sled |

D Listen and connect.

1.

b ed
sl ig

2.

p ed
b ig

3.

b ed
r ig

4.

r ed
tw ig

5.

b ed
p ig

6.

tw ed
r ig

E Trace and write.

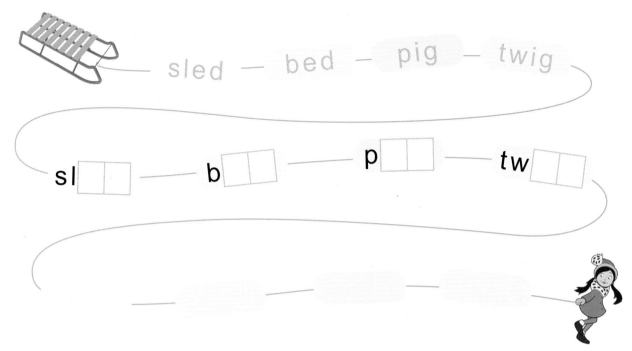

sled — bed — pig — twig

sl☐☐ — b☐☐ — p☐☐ — tw☐☐

F Look and write.

1. b + ☐ → big
   + ig → ☐

2. ☐ + ed → ☐
   sl + ☐ → sled

3. r + ☐ → ☐
   ☐ + ed → red

 G **Find and place the stickers.** stickers 2

1.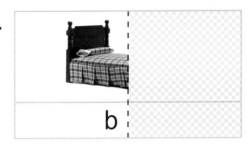

b

2.

sl

3.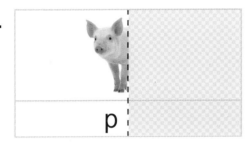

p

4.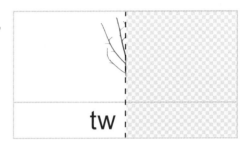

tw

 H **Look, circle, and write.**

1.

bed   sled   pig

You can see Santa Claus flying in a _____.

2.

twig   big   red

You can see white snow resting on the _____s.

A Trip on a Ship

■ **Listen to the story.**　　　■ **Listen and circle.**

 T13

The captain greets all the passengers. "Welcome aboard!"

1

A hen ties a hat under her **chin**.

chin

2

A seagull is flapping its **wings**.

3

wing

A little **chick** is following the mother hen.

4

chick

A duck is eating with its **bill**.

bill

The captain **winks** at the passengers.

wink

"Enjoy the trip!" the captain says.

trip

⑦

All the passengers are happy to be on the ship.

⑧

1 Word Families -**in** & -**ing**

A Listen and repeat.

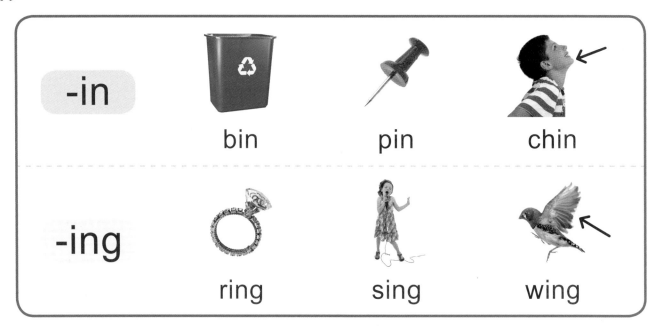

-in

bin pin chin

-ing

ring sing wing

B Listen and circle.

1. bin

2. sing

3. pin

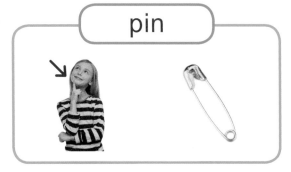

4. ring

C Listen, find, and write.

1.
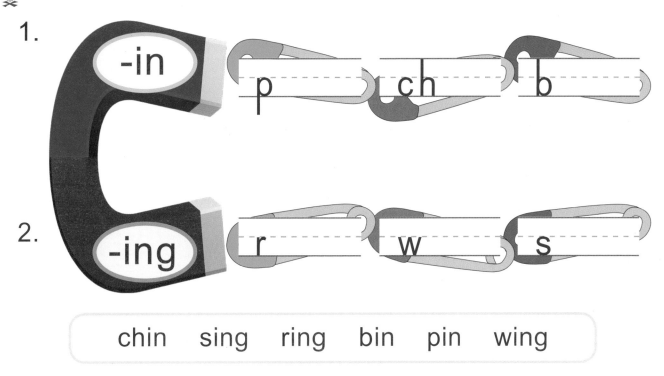

-in p _____ ch _____ b _____

2.
-ing r _____ w _____ s _____

chin   sing   ring   bin   pin   wing

D Listen, trace, and write.

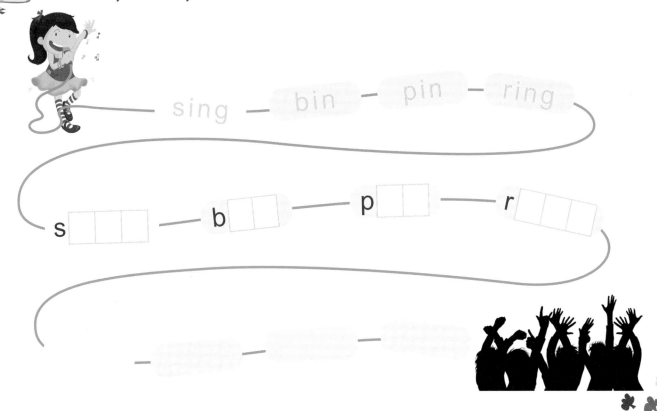

sing – bin – pin – ring

s ☐☐☐   b ☐☐   p ☐☐   r ☐☐

E Look, choose, and trace.

1. bin | pin

2. wing | sing

3. ring | wing

4. chin | bin

5. sing | ring

6. pin | chin

F Read and check.

1. It is a red pin.

2. It is a gold ring.

3. A girl is singing.

 Find and place the stickers.

-in

-ing

H **Look, circle, and write.**

1.

   bin   chin   pin

   _____

   A hen ties a hat under her _____ .

2.

   ring   sing   wing

   _____

   A seagull is flapping its _____ s.

2 Word Families -**ick** & -**ill**

A Listen and repeat.

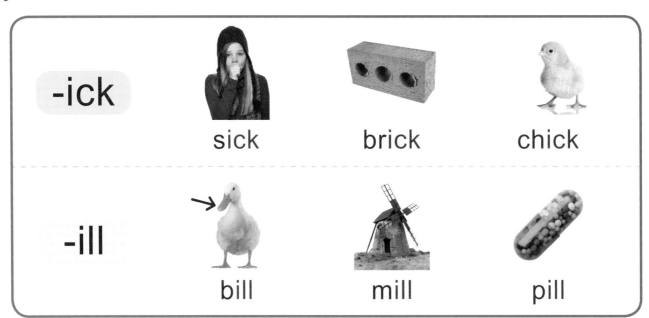

-ick

sick   brick   chick

-ill

bill   mill   pill

B Listen, write, and match.

1. ch _____ •   •

2. p _____ •   •

3. m _____ •   •

4. s _____ •   •

C Listen, find, and write.

1.

-ick

_____

- - - - - - - - - - - - - -

_____

2.

-ill

_____

- - - - - - - - - - - - - -

_____

D Listen and solve the maze.

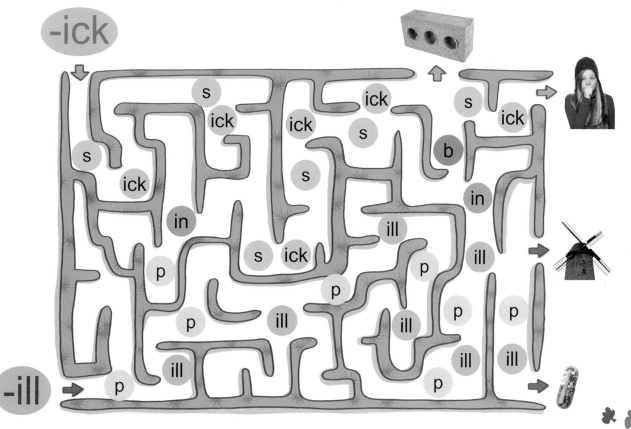

E Look and write.

1.

b +  → bill

+ ill →

2.

+ ick →

br + → brick

3.

ch + → chick

+ ick →

4.

p + →

+ ill → pill

F Read and circle.

1. A sick chick has a brick.

2. A duck pecks the pill with its bill in the mill.

 G **Find and place the stickers.** stickers 2

1.

s	
br	

2.

p	
m	

 H **Look, circle, and write.**

1.

chick   kick   brick

A little _____ is following the mother hen.

2.

bill   mill   pill

A duck is eating with its _____.

3 Word Families -**ink** & -**ip**

 A Listen and repeat.

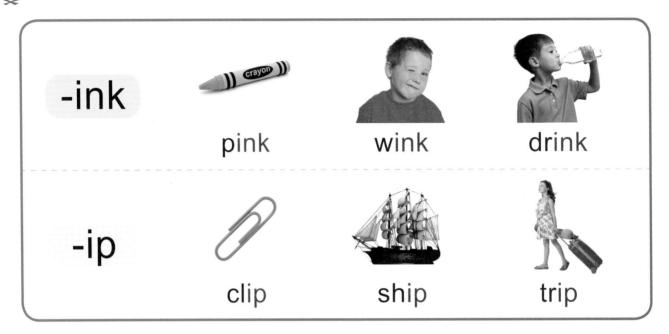

-ink

pink   wink   drink

-ip

clip   ship   trip

B Listen and circle the same ending sounds.

1.

-ink

pink

wink

clip

2.

-ip

drink

ship

trip

C Listen, find, and write.

1.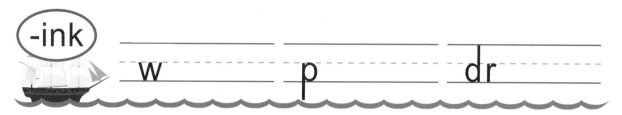

(-ink)

w _____ p _____ dr _____

2.

(-ip)

cl _____ tr _____ sh _____

> pink   ship   wink   trip   clip   drink

D Listen, trace, and write.

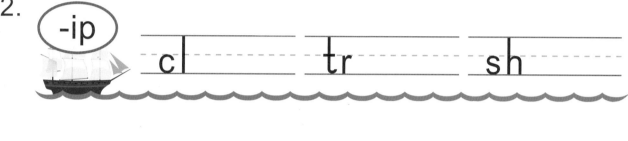

trip – pink – ship – drink

tr☐☐ – p☐☐☐ – sh☐☐ – dr☐☐☐

E Look and connect.

1.

tr ink
w ip

2.

dr ink
sh ip

3.

cl ink
dr ip

4.

tr ink
w ip

5.

cl ink
p ip

6.

cl ink
w ip

F Look, match, and write.

1.

2.

3.

4.

-ink

-ip

p   dr   tr   sh

G **Color the -ink words in** pink **and the -ip words in** blue.

pink	drink	
clip		ship
	wink	trip

H **Look, circle, and write.**

1.

drink   wink   ship

_____

The captain _____s at the passengers.

2.

trip   clip   pink

_____

"Enjoy the _____!" the captain says.

Phonics Song

 Sing a song.

Let's tap the beat!

A P ap ap   cap nap clap
A B ab ab   cab lab crab
A T at at   cat hat mat
A N an an   can man pan

E T et et   net pet wet
E N en en   hen ten den
E L L ell ell   bell well shell
E D ed ed   bed red sled

I N in in   bin pin chin
I G ig ig   big pig twig
I C K ick ick   sick brick chick
I N G ing ing   ring sing wing

Now you read all 36 words!

Unit 1 Hide-and-Seek

p. 2~5

cat    gold   web

box   under

hungry

p. 6

B 1. c 2. c 3. g 4. g 5. g 6. c

p. 7

C

D 1. c-at   2. g-old   3. c-ake
   4. g-um 5. g-love 6. c-up

p. 8

E 1. cup 2. gold 3. gum 4. cake

F 1. c, cup 2. g, glove
   3. c, cat 4. g, gum

p. 9

G c. 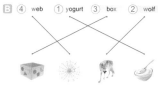   g.

H 1. Cat 2. gold

p. 10

B ④ web ① yogurt ③ box ② wolf

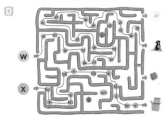

p. 11

C 1. web wolf (yo-yo) box

   2. wet (box) yogurt web

D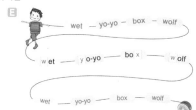

p. 12

E wet — yo-yo — box — wolf
   wet — yo-yo — box — wolf
   wet — yo-yo — box — wolf

F 1. web   2. box
   3. yogurt 4. yo-yo

p. 13

G 1. wolf 2. yo-yo 3. box 4. wet

H 1. web 2. box

p. 14

B 3 → 5 → 6 → 2 → 1 → 4

p. 15

C 1. up   2. hungry 3. umbrella
   4. jump 5. run   6. under

D

run hungry (jump)
(jump) (umbrella) (up)
(up) under hungry

p. 16

E 1. under 2. hungry 3. jump

F 1. u+p → up 2. r+u+n → run
   3. j+u+m+p → jump

p. 17

G

H 1. under 2. hungry

Unit 2 A Day at the Beach

p. 18~21

crab   cap   man

pants   wag   hat

p. 22

B 1.   2.   3.   4.

p. 23

C 1. cab, crab, lab
   2. cap, clap, nap

D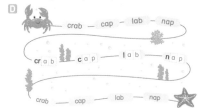

crab — cap — lab — nap
crab — cap — lab — nap
crab — cap — lab — nap

p. 24

E 1. cap 2. cab 3. lab
   4. nap 5. crab 6. clap

F 1.   2.   3.   4.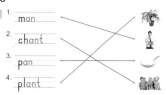

p. 25

G 1. ab 2. ap

H 1. crab 2. cap

p. 26

B 1. man
   2. chant
   3. pan
   4. plant

p. 27

C 1. man 2. plant

D

p. 28

E 1. c+an → can
   2. pl+ant → plant
   3. ch+ant → chant
   4. p+an → pan

F 1. -an A (man) has a (can) and a (pan).
   2. -ant A man (chants) about (pants) and (plants).

p. 29

G

can   pants
man   pan
       plant   chant

H 1. man 2. pant

p. 30

B 1. tag, flag 2. hat, mat

p. 31

C 1. flag, tag, wag 2. mat, hat, cat

D

p. 32

E 1. h-at 2. m-at 3. t-ag
   4. fl-ag 5. c-at 6. w-ag

F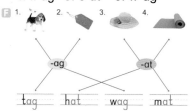

tag   hat   wag   mat

p. 33

G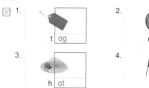

1. t ag   2. m at
3. h at   4. fl ag

H 1. wag 2. hat

Unit 3 It's the Holiday Season

p. 34~37

pet  ten  bell

nest  sled twig

p. 38

B 1. -et 2. -et 3. -en
4. -en 5. -et 6. -en

p. 39

C 1. net, pet, wet 2. ten, den, hen

D (hen) ten net
(wet) (den) (hen)
pet net (wet)

p. 40

E 1. net 2. ten 3. hen 4. wet

F 1. en, den 2. et, net
3. en, ten 4. et, pet

p. 41

G -et. 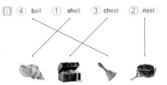 -en.

H 1. pet 2. ten

p. 42

B ④ bell ① shell ③ chest ② nest

p. 43

C 1. well 2. chest

D
-ell
-est

p. 44

E 1. shell 2. chest 3. well

F 1. 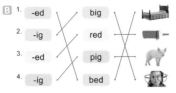 2. 3.

p. 45

G

bell	shell	
test		nest
	well	chest

H 1. bell 2. nest

p. 46

B 1. -ed big
2. -ig red
3. -ed pig
4. -ig bed

p. 47

C 1. bed, sled, red
2. twig, pig, big

D 1. sl-ed 2. p-ig 3. b-ig
4. tw-ig 5. b-ed 6. r-ed

p. 48

E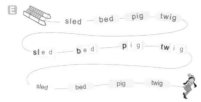
sled — bed — pig — twig
sl e d — b e d — p i g — tw i g
sled — bed — pig — twig

F 1. b+ig → big 2. sl+ed → sled
3. r+ed → red

p. 49

G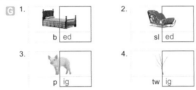
1. b|ed 2. sl|ed
3. p|ig 4. tw|ig

H 1. sled 2. twig

Unit 4 A Trip on a Ship

p. 50~53

chin wing chick

bill wink trip

p. 54

B 1.  2. 3. 4.

p. 55

C 1. pin, chin, bin
2. ring, wing, sing

D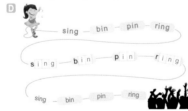
sing — bin — pin — ring
s i n g — b i n — p i n — r i n g
sing — bin — pin — ring

p. 56

E 1. pin 2. wing 3. ring
4. bin 5. sing 6. chin

F 1. 2. 3.

p. 57

G -in. -ing.

H 1. chin 2. wing

p. 58

B 1. chick 2. pill 3. mill 4. sick

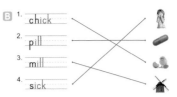

p. 59

C 1. brick 2. bill

D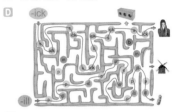
-ick
-ill

p. 60

E 1. b+ill → bill
2. br+ick → brick
3. ch+ick → chick
4. p+ill → pill

F 1. -ick A (sick)(chick) has a (brick)
2. -ill A duck pecks the (pill) with its (bill) in the (mill)

p. 61

G 1. ick 2. ill

H 1. chick 2. bill

p. 62

B 1. pink, wink 2. ship, trip

p. 63

C 1. wink, pink, drink
2. clip, trip, ship

D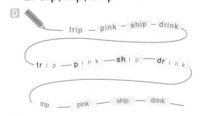
trip — pink — ship — drink
tr i p — p i n k — sh i p — dr i n k
trip — pink — ship — drink

p. 64

E 1. tr-ip 2. sh-ip 3. dr-ink
4. w-ink 5. p-ink 6. cl-ip

F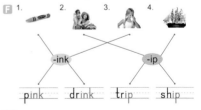
1. 2. 3. 4.
-ink -ip
pink drink trip ship

p. 65

G

pink	drink	
clip		ship
	wink	trip

H 1. wink 2. trip

stickers 1

stickers 2

stickers 3

yo-yo

umbrella

wolf   box   wet

stickers 1

stickers 2

ab

ap

ag   at   at   ag

stickers 1

stickers 2

ed   ig

ig   ed

stickers 1

stickers 2

ill   ick